Copyright © 2023 Mary Fitzgerald & Teekwa Scarborough
THE COURSE CREATION GPS

First Edition, September 2023

All rights reserved.
Produced in the United States of America
Paper Back/color

Unless written permission to reprint is secured, reproduction by any medium, including electronic, is strictly prohibited. To secure permission to reprint any section of this book contact Mary Fitzgerald and/or Teekwa Scarborough.

ISBN 978-1-7330781-3-9

Dynamicbusinessbuilding.com
and Ladytycoons.com

A NOTE FROM THE AUTHORS
TO THE UP AND COMING ENTREPRENEURS

Hello and WELCOME to the **Course Creation GPS**. You have no idea how excited we are that you took this GIANT step forward and decided to get started on the creation of your very own course.
Some of you, like us, have probably been thinking about it for years. Now you are on your way. Just wait until you are finished. You are going to feel so amazing and SO PROUD of yourself, and you will deserve every bit of it!

Having been in several of our own businesses over decades, we came together, by chance, at a marketing conference in New Jersey. A few of us ladies, all in our own businesses, would gather for lunch and talk about all the things that we were doing in and for our businesses. It was "social networking" the old-fashioned way, and it was fun. More than just fun though, it made us realize that we knew enough,...enough to help other up-and-coming entrepreneurs get going in their own online businesses, by starting with an online course.

Our first venture into the online course world was a **21-Day Business Building Challenge**, and boy did WE end up learning a lot! We learned that 21 days was pretty long for a challenge. We also learned that we were so excited to help others and so passionate about what we wanted to teach, that we may have, just a little bit, (more like a whole lot!) overwhelmed a few of our students.

That is how we came to create the **Course Creation GPS** course. If you put an address into the GPS in your car or on your phone, it gives you the directions to your destination turn by turn...one step at a time. It DOES NOT tell you everything to do all at once. That is the big lesson we learned from our first course, NO ONE can learn everything they need to know all at once, but ANYONE can learn anything if they take it one step at a time.

So, thank you for being here. We sincerely appreciate that you put your trust in us to help guide you as you begin this wonderful journey. Our goal is to help you, step by step, move through the process and we literally can't wait to see you at the finish line :)
So, thank you for being here, and taking this STEP in the direction of your very own online course. We sincerely appreciate that you put your trust in us to help guide you as you begin this wonderful journey. Our goal is to help you, step by step, move through the process and we literally can't wait to see you at the finish line :)

Teekwa and Mary

Teekwa and Mary
Dynamicbusinessbuilding.com
and Ladytycoons.com

TABLE OF CONTENTS

one

MODULE 1
- [ ] **INTRODUCTION**
  Welcome and Mindset 6-7
- [ ] **UNCOVERING YOUR GENIUS**
  How to decide what to teach 10
- [ ] **VALIDATING YOUR COURSE IDEA**
  Make sure there is a market for your idea 17

MODULE 2
- [ ] **NAIL DOWN YOUR NICHE**
  What target market do you want to serve 23

MODULE 3
- [ ] **YOUR IDEAL CLIENT**
  Who's your business bestie 31
- [ ] **A LETTER FROM YOUR IDEAL CLIENT**
  A glimpse into the future 38

two

MODULE 4
- [ ] **ONE SENTENCE FOR SUCCESS**
  The mini blueprint of your course 44
- [ ] **THE CLIENT JOURNEY - FOR YOUR COURSE**
  What Problem Will You Solve 50

three

MODULE 5
- [ ] **CREATING THE COURSE OUTLINE**
  Filling in the details - week-by-week 58
- [ ] **THE VALUE LADDER**
  The client journey for your BUSINESS 65

four

MODULE 6
- [ ] **BRAINSTORMING YOUR OFFER**
  And what's in a Name 81-83
- [ ] **ORGANIC MARKETING**
  Spreading the word without spending a dime 85
- [ ] **THE BETA LAUNCH**
  Taking a leap of faith - YOU"VE GOT THIS! 90

five

- [ ] **CONCLUSION**
  What comes next 93
- [ ] **VALUABLE RESOURCES**
  Everything you need to know (for now) 94

Dynamic Business Building © 2023

DOCUMENTS & WORKSHEETS
WHERE TO FIND THEM

1. Uncover your Genius/Superpower *12-16*
2. Validating Your Course Idea *19-21*
3. Nail Down Your Niche *25-26*
4. Passions and Interests Worksheets *27-29*
5. Ideal Client Questions *33-37*
6. Ideal Client Letter *40*
7. Pain Points and Desires Worksheets *46-47*
8. Which Problem Will You Solve *48-49*
9. The Client Journey Worksheets *52-54*
10. Weekly Course Outline Worksheets *60-64*
11. The Value Ladder Examples *67-75*
12. Brainstorming Your Offer *81-82*
13. Naming Your Course *83-84*
14. Conversation Starter Questions *85-86*
15. Simple Content Creation Examples *87-89*
16. The Beta Launch *90-91*

Dynamic Business Building © 2023

COURSE CREATION GPS

WELCOME TO THE COURSE CREATION GPS!

Why a GPS? *Because it guides you step by step*

G is for GATHER
In SECTION 1 of the course and workbook, the lessons are dedicated to gathering information. You will be working on how to uncover your strengths, talents and GENIUS. Next, there are some great exercises on discovering exactly WHO you want to work with. Then you will narrow down your focus on exactly WHAT you want to teach and validate whether or not there is a viable market for your chosen subject.

P is for PLAN
Section 2 of the course will go much deeper into the planning. Here you answer some very important questions and create the ONE SENTENCE that all of your future marketing will be based upon. You will clarify "What problem" you are going to solve for your clients and how to get them the results they desire.

S is for STEP-BY-STEP
Section 3 gets into the details, as you lay out the modules and lessons for your course and decide how you want to deliver them. But wait...there's more! We don't want you to create your course and call it a day, we want to show you what is possible. We want you to create an online business...that is why we introduce the Value Ladder.

STEP-BY-STEP Continues in Section 4
Here you will put it all together, Brainstorm Your Offer and learn "What's In A Name". We also show you a super easy way to create an abundance of relevant content to use in marketing organically = free ;)...not to mention the all important BETA LAUNCH.

Resources
Section 5 doesn't have a letter attached, but here we talk about what's next and it does have a bunch of amazing RESOURCES for you to check out. Many are free, and all meant to help make building your business as easy and stress-free as possible.

COURSE CREATION GPS

MINDSET

>
>
> *"PEOPLE OVERESTIMATE WHAT THEY CAN ACCOMPLISH IN ONE YEAR AND UNDERESTIMATE WHAT THEY CAN ACCOMPLISH IN TEN"*
>
> — TONY ROBBINS

Mind Your Mindset
Remember EVERYONE starts at the beginning.
Answer these questions to help create a positive mindset.

1 – What do you want to accomplish with this course?

2 – What do you want to accomplish in the next year?

3 – Why do you believe you CAN accomplish this?

4 – What do you want to accomplish in the next 5 years?

5 – Why do you believe you CAN accomplish this?

6 – What do you think some of the obstacles will be that could get in your way?

7 – What can you do to minimize each of the obstacles?

Obstacle	Solution
_____	_____
_____	_____
_____	_____
_____	_____
_____	_____

SECTION ONE
workbook

GATHER

Dynamic Business Building © 2023

GATHER
MODULE 1

UNCOVER YOUR *workbook* GENIUS

Dynamic Business Building © 2023

LESSON ONE

UNCOVER YOUR GENIUS

SECTION INTRODUCTION

Have you ever been told by your friends or family that "you are so good at that, you should start a business"? Do you easily solve certain problems for others that they feel are too hard to understand? Do you find yourself so lost in an activity that you forget to eat?
These are all signs of you working with your GENIUS!

Everyone has special talents, things that they can do effortlessly, that are difficult for most others. We don't see it as our genius though, we just take it for granted and think "it's no big deal" or "of course, doesn't everyone know how to do that?"
The truth is, they don't. YOU are the expert in that. YOU can be the one who helps them learn it too!

In this module, there are a bunch of great questions to help focus in on those things that you do well, and LOVE to do. When you finish, you will have a much better sense of what you can do to help others.

As you go through the questions, circle the things that keep coming up in your answers. Are there any patterns? Does the same answer show up multiple times? Jot a few of these ideas down in the space provided and think about how you can serve people with your talents... **That is your true GENIUS.** Once you know what you are good at, and love to do, it will help clarify what it is you want to teach to others in your course.

You are about to learn some stuff about yourself that you may never have realized before...*have FUN :)*

UNCOVER YOUR GENIUS

HOW TO DECIDE WHAT TO TEACH

What have you been complimented on?
What were the skills needed

What have you been recognized for?
What were the skills needed

What have others said you do well or are good at?
What were the skills needed

UNCOVER YOUR GENIUS

HOW TO DECIDE WHAT TO TEACH

What do you enjoy doing most, if you have a free day?
What were the skills needed

What would you do if money were no object?
What were the skills needed

What have been the jobs or roles that you have held, that you have enjoyed the most?
What were the skills needed

UNCOVER YOUR GENIUS

HOW TO DECIDE WHAT TO TEACH

What comes easy to you, yet seems difficult for others?
What were the skills needed

What have people told you to monetize, produce or turn into a service?
What were the skills needed

What have you seen others complain about how hard it was, when you thought, "really, all you have to do is…XYZ"? What were the skills needed

UNCOVER YOUR GENIUS

HOW TO DECIDE WHAT TO TEACH

If you are so engrossed in a job/task that you lose track of time or forget to eat...What is it that you are doing? What were the skills needed

What are 3 specific skills you have developed that make you successful at what you do?

What are the 2 things that you do in your business that make you the happiest and at the same time make the most money?

UNCOVER YOUR GENIUS

HOW TO DECIDE WHAT TO TEACH

Write down the story that was a turning point in your life that lead you to today, in relation to your niche. What were the "epiphany" moments…experiences, rough times, good times…times when you had to shift - to make a decision one way or another. This is your Transformational Story or your Hero's Journey.
This will help people know you, like you, and relate to you more easily.

What are some of the things that keep showing up?

1. _____
2. _____
3. _____

My True Genius is: _____

_____

VALIDATE YOUR COURSE
workbook
IDEA

Dynamic Business Building © 2023

LESSON TWO

VALIDATING YOUR COURSE IDEA

SECTION INTRODUCTION

Did you ever have an amazing idea and think "this is going to make me millions of dollars," only to put it out into the marketplace and just hear crickets, because nobody wanted it? That does not feel good : (That is the last thing we want for you, so this module is all about validating your course idea. Making sure that somebody out there wants what you are offering, somebody is interested in the topic, and somebody has been **asking the question** that you answer.

Many people think that competition in business is a bad thing, but a certain amount of competition is actually a good thing. If *nobody* is searching for what you are offering or asking for what you are answering, then you will just become frustrated.

So go to each one of the platforms listed below, type in your topic idea or phrase, and see what comes up. In places like Google and Amazon, which are search platforms, as you type in your word(s), you will start to see other suggestions pop up...*WRITE THESE DOWN*...they are marketing gold because this is EXACTLY what people are searching for...in their own words. Then YOU can use those words in your content and marketing.

Using "Answer the Public.com" is fun. Just type in your word or phrase, and you will get EVERYTHING that people are searching for in Google using those words. It will show up as a circular graph, which is cool because you can see that the darker the color green, the more it was searched. But for ease of reading and printing, you can choose the "DATA" button and see the information in list form. You can check out the data in several different categories, but you can only do 2 searches per day, so choose wisely ;)

You will likely discover some words that people use to ask for your product or service that you never thought of before, or the way that they phrase a question may be different than what you have been thinking. This process will help you find out **exactly** what your prospective clients are actually asking for and you will then be able to answer exactly what it is that they need. Solve their problem and you will succeed.

VALIDATING YOUR COURSE IDEA

Facebook Pages (Write down the owner's name if possible)

Facebook Groups (Write down the owner's name if possible)

Amazon Books

What are some of the questions, ideas or problems that came up that YOU can solve?
_____
_____
_____
_____
_____

VALIDATING YOUR COURSE IDEA

Google

Google Trends

Instagram (Write down the owner's name if possible)

What are some of the questions, ideas or problems that came up that YOU can solve?
_____
_____
_____
_____
_____

VALIDATING YOUR COURSE IDEA

Podcast - Podbooker.com

Blog Posts (Write down the owner's name if possible)

Answerthepublic.com

What are some of the questions, ideas or problems that came up that YOU can solve?

_____
_____
_____

If nothing came up in your searches...try a different word or phrase or note what DID come up that was closely related to your idea. Otherwise, you may have to re-think your idea.

GATHER
MODULE 2

NAIL DOWN YOUR *workbook* NICHE

MODULE TWO

CHOOSING YOUR NICHE

SECTION INTRODUCTION

You may know WHAT you want to teach, but you must also know WHO you want to teach it to. In this module you will work on choosing where you want to focus and determine exactly what **Niche** you are going to serve.

There are 3 BIG Niches: Health, Wealth and Relationships. Your niche should fall into one of these, if you want it to be successful. But these categories are TOO BIG for the small business owner, so we have to drill down and focus on a smaller "piece" of the giant niche. And best to go down another level (or two), just to get more specific. They say there are "Riches in Niches"!

For example, in the **Wealth Niche**, you can narrow it down to **Real Estate**. Then you can narrow it down again to **Flipping Houses for Profit**. You can continue to narrow it down, (**ex. Flipping Houses for Beginners)** until you know exactly what you want to teach and to whom - Your Ideal Client. (That's a lesson for a different day!)

It's not only important to have a good idea, but it also has to be something that you love and are good at. You don't want to put your heart into creating something that you don't love. And it is more difficult to be successful at something you are not good at. Plus, if there is no market for it, you will be wasting your precious time.

However...when you put those three things together -
something that you're good at - something you have a passion for - and something that has a hot market - then you have discovered your PERFECT PRODUCT ZONE, also known as Your ZONE OF GENIUS!

NAIL DOWN YOUR NICHE

FINDING YOUR NICHE
YOUR CORE/FOUNDATIONAL PRODUCT

PASSION	OPPORTUNITY
A hobby (knitting, painting)	High demand – a lot of people searching for it
Something you have an interest in (horseback riding)	Is there a NEED in the marketplace
Something you have experience with (acne)	Where are people spending their money?
Something you enjoy talking about (basketball)	It's a Hot topic - What is selling NOW
Something you learned very well or easily (Spanish)	There's a proven model that you can follow
Something you can help people with (weight loss)	Pain points & desires – what people want/need
Something you love talking about (science, pirates)	People are spending money on your niche idea

---

**THE PERFECT ZONE =
PASSION + OPPORTUNITY**

NAIL DOWN YOUR NICHE

3 MARKETS THAT WILL NEVER DIE

GIANT CATEGORIES

HEALTH	WEALTH	RELATIONSHIPS
- Weight loss - General fitness - Muscle building - Supplements - Medical conditions	- Make money - Save money/ - budgeting - Stock Market - Business marketing - Network marketing	- Online dating - Marriage advice - Child raising advice - Divorce advice - Blended families

NICHE=ONE MORE LEVEL DEEP

Ex. Dating advice – "The Kiss Test"
Ex. Weight loss – "Keto for Keeps"
Ex. Budget – "Cut out Starbucks and buy your first house"

NAIL DOWN YOUR NICHE

FILL IN THE CHART BELOW WITH YOUR IDEAS AND RESEARCH

PASSIONS & INTEREST	ARE YOU GOOD AT IT?	IS THERE A MARKET FOR IT?

ADD A *HOT MARKET* TO YOUR *PASSION/INTEREST* AND *SKILLS* AND GET YOUR …

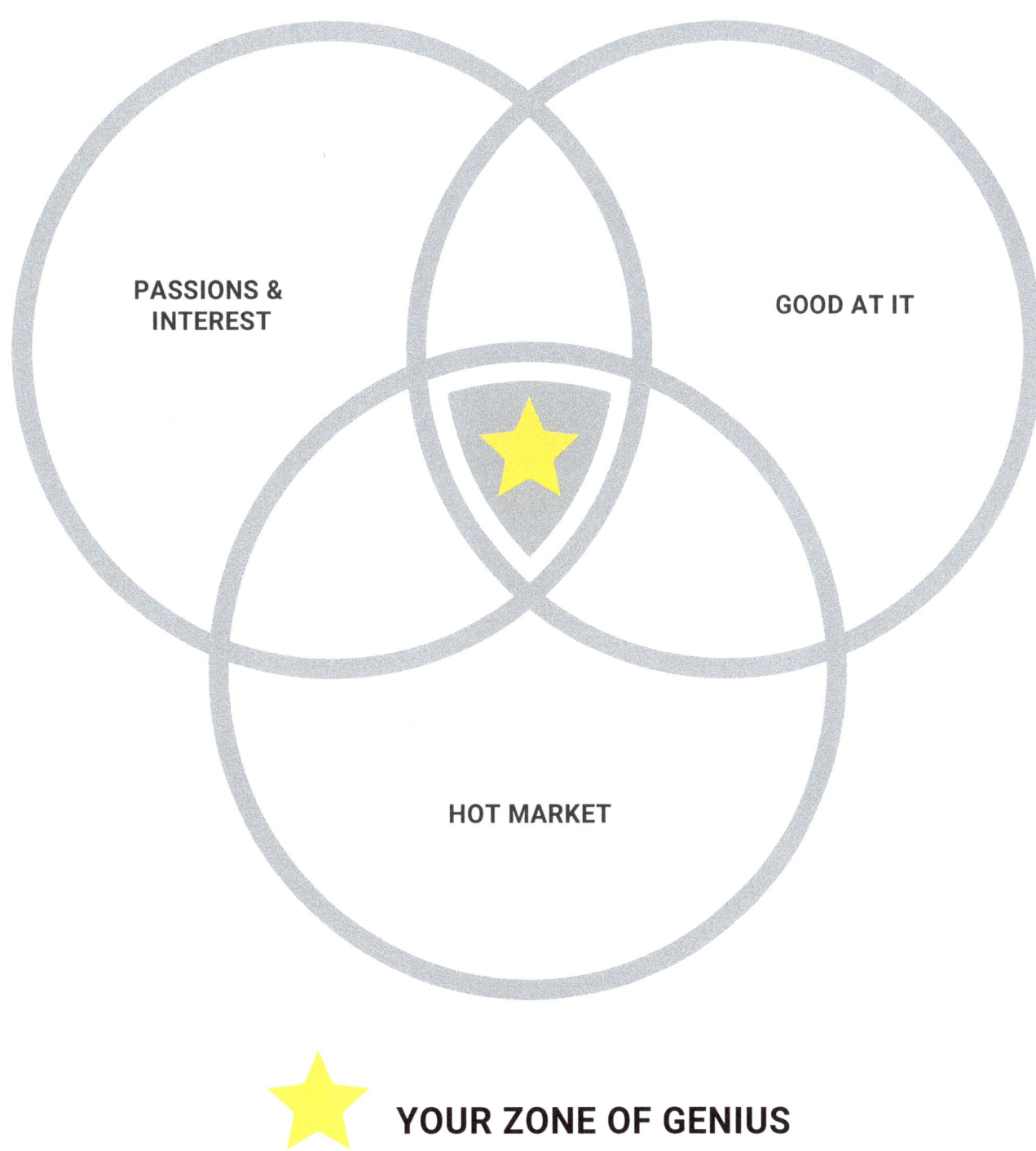

YOUR TURN... FILL IN THE BLANKS

ADD A *HOT MARKET* TO YOUR *PASSION/INTEREST* AND *SKILLS* AND GET YOUR ...

⭐ WHAT IS YOUR ZONE OF GENIUS

_____

GATHER
MODULE 3

YOUR IDEAL
workbook
CLIENT

Dynamic Business Building © 2023

LESSON ONE

YOUR IDEAL CLIENT

SECTION INTRODUCTION

Everyone who starts a new business, or creates a course, wants the same thing... CUSTOMERS (or clients, or patients). The biggest mistake is that they think either, "I'll take anyone that has a wallet and a pulse" OR, "I want to help EVERYONE!"
Both of those ideas are too broad to market to. If that is the message you put out, it will get lost in the noisy, crowded marketplace.

What you really need to know is exactly **WHO** your ideal client is. **WHO** is it that you would love to work with.

If you already have a business and have worked with some amazing people, just look back at which client(s) or customer(s) you absolutely loved working with and why. If you could multiply any client by one hundred or one thousand, who would that be? And what is it, specifically, that you LIKED about working with them?

If you are not sure who your ideal client is, then this module will be of tremendous value to you. There is a list of very specific questions you are going to go through, and the answers will help you determine who it is you want to work with, why you want to work with them, and why they would want to work with you!

This information will be immensely helpful as you begin to market with intention. Once you determine who your ideal client is... everything you do, everything you market, every headline that you create, and every post that you put out, is going to be focused on attracting your Ideal Client and solving their problem.

So this is a really important lesson, as well as a lot of fun. When you get to the end you will know exactly who your ideal client is.
Enjoy the process, we'll see you on the other side :)

YOUR IDEAL CLIENT

Think carefully about WHO you want to serve and answer all these questions with them in mind. The more you can get into the mind of your Ideal Client, the better you will understand their desires and needs. Then you will be able to help them solve the problems they have, in relation to your niche, product or service..
The great thing is that you get to CHOOSE who you want to work with!

GIVE HIM/HER A NAME TO MAKE THIS REAL. WHAT IS THEIR NAME?

WHAT IS THE AGE OF YOUR IDEAL CLIENT?

WHAT IS THEIR GENDER?

WHAT IS THEIR RELATIONSHIP STATUS?

DO THEY HAVE CHILDREN OR NOT?

WHAT TYPE OF CAREER DO THEY HAVE?

WHERE DOES YOUR IDEAL CLIENT LIVE? WHICH STATE OR COUNTRY?

DO THEY LIVE IN A HOUSE, CONDO, OR APARTMENT. DO THEY RENT OR OWN?

DO THEY LIVE IN THE CITY, COUNTRY OR SUBURBS?

DESCRIBE THEIR TYPICAL DAILY ROUTINE DURING THE WEEK DAYS.

YOUR IDEAL CLIENT

HOW DO THEY SPEND THEIR WEEKENDS? RELAXING OR WORKING?

DOES YOUR IDEAL CLIENT TRAVEL?

WHAT IS YOUR IDEAL CLIENT INSECURE ABOUT IN THEIR LIVES RIGHT NOW?

WHAT DO THEY FEEL CONFIDENT AND SECURE ABOUT IN THEIR LIVES RIGHT NOW?

WHAT KEEPS YOUR IDEAL CLIENT UP AT NIGHT?

WHAT ARE THEY STRESSED ABOUT WITH REGARD TO CAREER/BUSINESS?

WHAT ARE THEY STRESSED ABOUT WITH REGARD TO MONEY?

WHERE DO THEY WANT TO BE A YEAR FROM NOW? WHAT IS THEIR DESIRE?

IN WHAT AREAS ARE THEY REALLY TALENTED OR SKILLED?

WHY WOULD YOUR IDEAL CLIENT NOT BUY FROM YOU?

YOUR IDEAL CLIENT

HOW DOES YOUR IDEAL CLIENT MAKE THEIR BUYING DECISIONS?

WHAT FEAR OR FRUSTRATION WOULD THEY GLADLY PAY TO HAVE GO AWAY?

WHAT IS YOUR IDEAL CLIENT "MOVING AWAY FROM"? (EX. GET OUT OF DEBT)

WHAT ARE THEY "MOVING TOWARDS"? (EX. I WANT TO BE A MILLIONAIRE)

HOW DO THEY FEEL ABOUT THEMSELVES ON A PHYSICAL LEVEL?

HOW DO THEY FEEL ABOUT THEMSELVES ON A SPIRITUAL LEVEL?

HOW DO THEY FEEL ABOUT THEMSELVES ON AN INTELLECTUAL LEVEL?

HOW EDUCATED ARE THEY AND IN WHAT AREA(S) ARE THEY EDUCATED?

IS YOUR IDEAL CLIENT AN EXTROVERT OR AN INTROVERT?

DOES YOUR IDEAL CLIENT VALUE HEALTH?

YOUR IDEAL CLIENT

DOES YOUR IDEAL CLIENT VALUE LIFESTYLE?

DOES YOUR IDEAL CLIENT VALUE THEIR PERSONAL APPEARANCE?

DOES YOUR IDEAL CLIENT VALUE PERSONAL DEVELOPMENT?

WHAT PERSONAL DEVELOPMENT PRODUCTS/SERVICES DO THEY LIKE/USE?

WHAT IS YOUR IDEAL CLIENT'S DISPOSABLE INCOME?

DO THEY HAVE A GOOD RELATIONSHIP WITH MONEY?

.DO YOU HAVE ANY INTERESTS/HOBBIES THAT MIGHT CONNECT YOU WITH THEM?

WHAT OTHER COACHES/MENTORS MIGHT THEY BE INTERESTED IN WORKING WITH?

WHERE DO YOU WANT THEM TO GO & HOW DO YOU WANT THEM TO GROW?

WHAT TANGIBLE SKILL OR RESULT WILL THEY HAVE AFTER WORKING WITH YOU?

YOUR IDEAL CLIENT

ARE YOU STARTING TO BECOME CLEARER ON WHO HE/SHE IS?

WHO DO YOU SEE NOW AS YOUR TARGET MARKET AND IDEAL CLIENT?

WHY ARE YOU THE RIGHT COACH OR TEACHER FOR THIS IDEAL CLIENT?

WHY IS THIS PERSON THE BEST CLIENT FOR YOU TO COACH OR TEACH?

WELL DONE!...NOW FINISH LESSON 2 (YOUR CLIENT LETTER), THEN GO TO GOOGLE AND FIND A PICTURE OF YOUR IDEAL CLIENT. POST IT HERE AND/OR NEAR YOUR WORKSPACE...SO YOU KEEP THEM IN MIND WHEN CREATING ANY NEW COURSE, PRODUCTS AND/OR MARKETING :)

MY NAME IS:

YOUR CLIENT
workbook
LETTER

Dynamic Business Building © 2023

LESSON TWO

A LETTER FROM YOUR IDEAL CLIENT

SECTION INTRODUCTION

This is one of the most powerful and moving exercises you can do.

Complete the sentences in the letter below as if you were your ideal client. Take a moment to visualize what they look like, how the feel and what their answers to these questions would be.

Once you complete this letter, you will FEEL the transformation of your students. You will SEE what a difference you can make in their lives and you will finally UNDERSTAND how important it is for you to share your knowledge, through your online course!

No more procrastinating, people are wishing and hoping and praying for an answer...people are waiting for you.

Enough said.

PUTTING IT ALL TOGETHER...WHAT PROBLEM DID YOU SOLVE

A thank you letter from your Ideal Client
(As taught by Kim Walsh Phillips)

Dear _____,
(Your Name)

Before I found out about you
(Talk about what their life was like before they met you)

When I took your course, I realized
(Talk about what they discovered in your course)

That is when I
(Talk about what they did as a result of what they learned)

Now my life has changed because
(Talk about how their life has changed)

Thank you for
(What are they thankful for))

Sincerely, _____
(Your ideal client's name)

40
Dynamic Business Building © 2023

NOTES

EXAMPLE OF CLIENT LETTER:

Dear Linda,

Before I found out about you - I had a pretty good life, but I wanted a way to create some kind of course that would not only benefit me, financially, but would benefit many others in their own lives.

When I took your course, I realized - that even though I want to help everyone, I have to be more specific, at least at first. Then when I grow and become successful in that, I can expand to the next group of people to help. I also realized that I needed help, because I did not know where to start, or any of the technology to make this happen.

That is when I – decided to do the work and finally create my very own online course. A course to help people, just like me, get out of debt and live a more stress-free life.

And now my life has changed because – I can really see that I can make this happen. That all this information and passion that I have held in my mind and heart for years, can finally be organized in a way that I can share it with the world, make some money and make an impact by helping others better their life without the burden of debt!

Thank you for – showing me that it is possible and really, not even that hard to do, once you get the process down! I appreciate you being there to help me get it done.

Love,
Toni

SECTION TWO
workbook

PLAN

PLAN
MODULE 4

SENTENCE FOR SUCCESS
workbook

Dynamic Business Building © 2023

LESSON ONE

ONE SENTENCE FOR SUCCESS

SECTION INTRODUCTION

As humans, we usually make things more complicated than they need to be. In this module, we are working to simplify, clarify and
laser focus.
There are two very important things that you need to know about your potential client, customer, or patient.

What are their pain points and **what are their desires?**
What is it that keeps them up at night? What is it they worry about? What is it they wish they could change? And what is the change that they hope to accomplish?

Once you know what the problem is - what the pain point is - if you can answer that and show them how to get their desire, that is the formula for a winning course or a product.

This module goes through all of that, and helps you clarify exactly what the pain points and the desires are, of your potential clients

When you put together your Niche (Ideal client) with what Desire you can help them achieve, without the Pain Point they don't want, in a certain amount of Time...you have your One Sentence For Success. This sentence then becomes a mini blueprint of your entire course!

We are looking forward to seeing what you discover.

PAIN POINT & DESIRES

FILL IN THE CHART BELOW WITH YOUR IDEAS AND RESEARCH

PAIN POINTS
What are they worried about?
What keeps them up at night?

- The dog is an embarrassment in public
- They will get penalized for late taxes
- Not able to handle childbirth
- Missing their faithful dog or cat
- Not having the skills to write a book
- Their kids will be unhealthy

DESIRES
What is the opposite - the outcome they really want?

- They want the dog to behave in public
- Decrease stress knowing taxes are done
- A peaceful and relaxed birth
- A beautiful way to memorialize their pets
- The confidence to put their thoughts in a cohesive order
- Flexible, healthy & calm kids

THEY DON'T WANT THE PRODUCT → **THEY DO WANT THE RESULTS**

The Drill	The Hole
Lawn Mower	A Good Looking Lawn
Marriage Counselor	A Happy Relationship
A Fancy Shampoo	Luxurious, healthy & silky hair

THEY DON'T WANT
YOUR FACTS & FEATURES
SO YOU TEACH...

- How to train your dog
- How to run Facebook Ads
- How to do your own books
- The right exercise to workout

THEY DO WANT
YOUR BENEFITS & RESULTS
BUT YOU SELL...

- Not being embarrassed in public
- Having a steady stream of clients
- Save a lot of money
- Big muscles, Flat abs & Confidence

PAIN POINT & DESIRES

GETTING INTO THE MIND OF YOUR CLIENT

Pain Points may be similar to some of their objections **but they are not always the same.**

The opposite of their PAIN POINT is their DESIRE!
You have to know what their **PAIN POINTS** are so that you can show them how your product/service/course can **SOLVE** that pain point and change it into their **DESIRE**.

> *PAIN = What causes them trouble? What keeps them awake at night? What creates a barrier for them? What are they moving away from?*

> *DESIRE = Their Goals, What would bring them pleasure, the Outcome, Result or Transformation they really want. Usually the flip side of the PAIN.*

LIST YOUR IDEAL CLIENT'S PAIN POINTS AND DESIRES BELOW

PAIN	DESIRE
ex. Don't have enough clients	ex. A steady flow of new leads
_____	_____
_____	_____
_____	_____
_____	_____
_____	_____
_____	_____
_____	_____
_____	_____
_____	_____

WHICH PROBLEM ARE YOU GOING TO SOLVE?

COMPLETE THIS STATEMENT

I (do some action) ___*Niche*___ do/to ___*Desire*___
Without ___*Pain Point/Objection*___ in ___*Time Period*___

*Ex. I help newbie entrepreneurs build their online course, **without** even knowing what to teach, in 6 weeks.*

I (do some action) ___*Niche*___ do/to ___*Desire*___
While ___*Opposite of pain point*___ in ___*Time Period*___

*Ex. I teach dog groomers to add retail to their business, **while** still running their shop, in just 4 weeks.*

I (help) _____ do/to _____
Without _____ in (time)_____

I (teach) _____ do/to _____
Without _____ in (time)_____

I (inspire) _____ do/to _____
While _____ in (time)_____

I (guide) _____ do/to _____
While _____ in (time)_____

NOW IT'S YOUR TURN...
Fill in the blanks for your "Sentence For Success"

WHICH PROBLEM ARE YOU GOING TO SOLVE?

My Ideal Client/Niche: _____

What is their desire: _____

What is their pain point: _____

In what timeframe: _____

SO WHAT PROBLEM WILL YOU SOLVE?
Complete this statement

I _____ _____ do/to _____
     (Some action)   (Ideal client/niche)   (Desire)

without _____
             (Pain point/objection)

or while _____ *in* _____
       (Opposite of Pain point/objection)   (Time period)

Well done...you now have your

SENTENCE TO SUCCESS!

THE CLIENT JOURNEY
workbook

LESSON TWO

THE CLIENT JOURNEY FOR YOUR COURSE

SECTION INTRODUCTION

This module lays out the RESULT, The TRANSFORMATION, or the One Big PROMISE that your students will achieve, once they have completed your course.

Once you know their pain points and desires, you will be able to clearly state HOW YOU CAN HELP THEM...solve that pain point, fix that problem, and get to their desired outcome.

It is ALL ABOUT results, outcomes, and transformation.

Many times the result you are hoping to help your clients get, is one that you were able to achieve for yourself two, five, maybe ten years ago. But even if it is not, the steps are the same. Maybe you quit smoking or lost a lot of weight, or started your own daycare.

Think back to what it was like when you were in pain...the very beginning of your journey, or imagine what it is like for your clients right now.

Then write down all of the steps that you had to go through or they will have to go through, to get to the result. There will be some MAJOR steps and then some MINOR steps underneath them. The MAJOR steps become your Modules, the MINOR steps become the lessons in the modules.

We recommend about 4-8 modules to help your students/clients achieve one big result. Trying to solve too many problems or teaching too much information, leads to overwhelm. Overwhelming leads to inactivity, and never getting anything done.

No more digital dust...let's help your students/clients finish what they start and get the results they are looking for.

AN EXAMPLE OF THE STEPS (JOURNEY) NEEDED TO STARTING A HOME STAGING BUSINESS.

```
                                        6      ⚑
                                    5       HOME
                                4           STAGING
                            3               BUSINESS
                        2
                    1
START →
```

STEPS YOU TOOK OR YOUR CLIENTS NEED TO TAKE

1 TAKE A COURSE ON IT
Research different styles
Choose my preferred style
Signup for a close course

2 SET UP A BUSINESS
Research types of set-ups
Choose the best one for me
Have a lawyer create LLC

3 GET INVENTORY
Decide to RENT or OWN
Find where to rent stuff
Find best places to buy stuff

4 START MARKETING
Who to work with?
Realtors, Investors, Homeowners
Find out what they need... D.O.M

5 HIRE HELP
Where to find a good driver
Part time or Full time
What qualifications do I expect

6

7

8

NOW IT'S YOUR TURN.

Write out the steps (journey) needed to reach the end result, outcome or promise of your course.

```
                                            6
                                       5
                                   4
                               3
                           2                    YOUR ULTIMATE RESULT
                       1                        YOUR CLIENT'S ULTIMATE RESULT
                                                   (As taught by Russell Brunson)
   START →
```

STEPS YOU TOOK OR YOUR CLIENTS NEED TO TAKE

1 _____   **2** _____
   a.   a.
   b.   b.
   c.   c.

3 _____   **4** _____
   a.   a.
   b.   b.
   c.   c.

5 _____   **6** _____
   a.   a.
   b.   b.
   c.   c.

7 _____   **8** _____
   a.   a.
   b.   b.
   c.   c.

THEN...

EVERY STEP AND EVERY SUB-STEP BECOMES A PIECE OF CONTENT FOR YOUR MARKETING

        6   realtors vs. investors

        5   finding a good team

        4   best places to shop

        3   rent or buy furniture

        2   best business set-up

        1   how to find a course

START ⟶ types of home staging

Each step along the way can become a Facebook post, an Instagram story, a Youtube video, a TikTok, a Podcast topic, or a Blog post!
So you will always have plenty of things to talk and post about!

NOTES

SECTION THREE
workbook

STEP BY STEP

STEP BY STEP
MODULE 5

COURSE CREATION *workbook* OUTLINE

Dynamic Business Building © 2023

LESSON ONE

CREATING THE COURSE OUTLINE

SECTION INTRODUCTION

Now that you have all the STEPS of the journey laid out...you
can organize them all into the MODULES and LESSONS of your course.

You want to keep the information in a logical order, how will your student move from Point A - where they are now, to Point B, the result they want to achieve through your course.

Ideally, there should be about 4-8 modules. Too many modules and the student may get tired and overwhelmed. The course should help them achieve One Big Win, and then be complete. Once they see the great results from the first course, they will be asking you the magic question..."What else do you have? Always keep in mind, what is the next step for your clients. *(More on that in The Value Ladder section)*

The BIG steps along the journey become the modules and the LITTLE steps become the lessons under each module.

Go through each of the worksheets that follow and decide which ways you want to deliver your course material. There are several ways, and you can mix and match...video (live or recorded, ex: Zoom or Loom), Facebook (live or recorded), power point (you on camera or off), email, etc... and plan it all out, week by week. Remember, this is an outline, a plan, there is nothing written in stone-yet!

Once you have the steps outlined, and you have an idea of what documents, handouts or videos you want to include, you are ready to create your course. We don't recommend creating everything ahead of time, just the outline of what you want to teach. Then you'll be ready for your Beta Launch - which we talk about in another section. Enjoy the process :)

COURSE CREATION OUTLINE

CREATE A WEEK – BY – WEEK PLAN FOR YOUR COURSE

General Course Delivery Type: Live Videos, Videos, Power Point/Slides, Group Coaching, Email, Other.
TOPIC covered and how it will be
DELIVERED each week: Live Videos, Videos, PowerPoint/Slides, Group Coaching, Email, Other
TASKS to be assigned to the students and the
TOOLS you need to deliver the content: Worksheets, Downloads, Templates, Videos, etc...

Module # _____ Title: _____

Lesson # _____ Title: _____

TOPIC COVERED	DELIVERY METHOD	TASKS ASSIGNED	TOOLS NEEDED

Module # _____ Title: _____

Lesson # _____ Title: _____

TOPIC COVERED	DELIVERY METHOD	TASKS ASSIGNED	TOOLS NEEDED

COURSE CREATION OUTLINE

Module # _____   Title: _____
Lesson # _____   Title: _____

TOPIC COVERED	DELIVERY METHOD	TASKS ASSIGNED	TOOLS NEEDED

Module # _____   Title: _____
Lesson # _____   Title: _____

TOPIC COVERED	DELIVERY METHOD	TASKS ASSIGNED	TOOLS NEEDED

Module # _____   Title: _____
Lesson # _____   Title: _____

TOPIC COVERED	DELIVERY METHOD	TASKS ASSIGNED	TOOLS NEEDED

COURSE CREATION OUTLINE

Module # _____ Title: _____

Lesson # _____ Title: _____

TOPIC COVERED	DELIVERY METHOD	TASKS ASSIGNED	TOOLS NEEDED

Module # _____ Title: _____

Lesson # _____ Title: _____

TOPIC COVERED	DELIVERY METHOD	TASKS ASSIGNED	TOOLS NEEDED

Module # _____ Title: _____

Lesson # _____ Title: _____

TOPIC COVERED	DELIVERY METHOD	TASKS ASSIGNED	TOOLS NEEDED

COURSE CREATION OUTLINE

Module # _____ Title: _____

Lesson # _____ Title: _____

TOPIC COVERED	DELIVERY METHOD	TASKS ASSIGNED	TOOLS NEEDED

Module # _____ Title: _____

Lesson # _____ Title: _____

TOPIC COVERED	DELIVERY METHOD	TASKS ASSIGNED	TOOLS NEEDED

Module # _____ Title: _____

Lesson # _____ Title: _____

TOPIC COVERED	DELIVERY METHOD	TASKS ASSIGNED	TOOLS NEEDED

COURSE CREATION OUTLINE

Module # _____   Title: _____
Lesson # _____   Title: _____

TOPIC COVERED	DELIVERY METHOD	TASKS ASSIGNED	TOOLS NEEDED

Module # _____   Title: _____
Lesson # _____   Title: _____

TOPIC COVERED	DELIVERY METHOD	TASKS ASSIGNED	TOOLS NEEDED

Module # _____   Title: _____
Lesson # _____   Title: _____

TOPIC COVERED	DELIVERY METHOD	TASKS ASSIGNED	TOOLS NEEDED

YOUR VALUE LADDER
workbook

Dynamic Business Building © 2023

LESSON TWO

THE VALUE LADDER-
THE CUSTOMER JOURNEY FOR YOUR BUSINESS

SECTION INTRODUCTION

The Value Ladder - We call this the "New Business Plan".

Just like there was a Customer Journey for your course, there is a customer journey for your business.

You always want to know what the next step is for your students.
Very often, once they take your amazing course and get the result they were hoping to get, the next (magical) question is..."What else can I learn from you"?

You want to have an answer for that question! That's where the Value Ladder comes in. Here we will go through how to lead your clients through your business. From just learning about you, to taking that first step into your world and then ascending up the ladder to what you have next for them, so they can continue to work with you.

The higher you go up the ladder, the higher the value, the higher the price. At the bottom of the ladder may be a freebie (pdf, cheat sheet, guide), then you lead them to a course (mini or signature course, challenge), from there they can join your group coaching, then to a mastermind, or a live event, and maybe even a monthly membership!

Just like in music, the closer you get to the Rock Star, the more "valuable" the experience, the higher the ticket price. You can listen to a song on the radio, hear the song from the "cheap seats" at a concert or thoroughly enjoy it with your backstage pass. You are listening to the same song, but the experience and how it is delivered, is very different. The perceived value is higher and so is the cost.

YOU are the ROCK STAR of your business. The closer your students/clients are working with you, the higher the value and the higher the price.

Following are several examples of Value Ladders for different types of businesses. Then there is a blank Value Ladder for you to fill out for your business.

This is the easiest business plan you will ever create...Have fun!

THE VALUE LADDER

(As taught by Russell Brunson)

GENERIC

VALUE ↑

- **Lead Magnet** — FREE
  - *A PDF, cheat sheet, tip sheet, guide, template, video, free sample, etc…*
- **Entry Product** — DIY
- **Next Level Product** — DWY
- **High Level Product** — DFY

$ → $ → $ CONTINUITY PROGRAM
A Continuity program happens automatically on a regular basis… weekly, monthly, bi-weekly, yearly, etc…

PRICE →

THE VALUE LADDER
FOR RETAIL PRODUCTS

VALUE ↑

The Next Logical Thing
(Entire "Get back to health" package with video coaching or training or workbook)

The Next Logical Thing
(Purchase 6 bottles of Vitamin C for a special price or buy a different Vitamin)

Item They Wanted
(Purchase a bottle of Vitamin C)

Free Gift
(Free sample of Vitamin C)

$ → $ → $
CONTINUITY PROGRAM
(Monthly supply of Vitamins)

PRICE →

THE VALUE LADDER

FOR A VIRTUAL ASSISTANT

VALUE ↑

- Free Checklist/ Evaluation
- Introductory Service
- Increase of Services Offered/ On-site Training
- Take Over Admin Duties

$ → $ → $

MONTHLY MAINTENANCE RETAINER

PRICE →

THE VALUE LADDER
FOR INFORMATION/ DIGITAL PRODUCTS

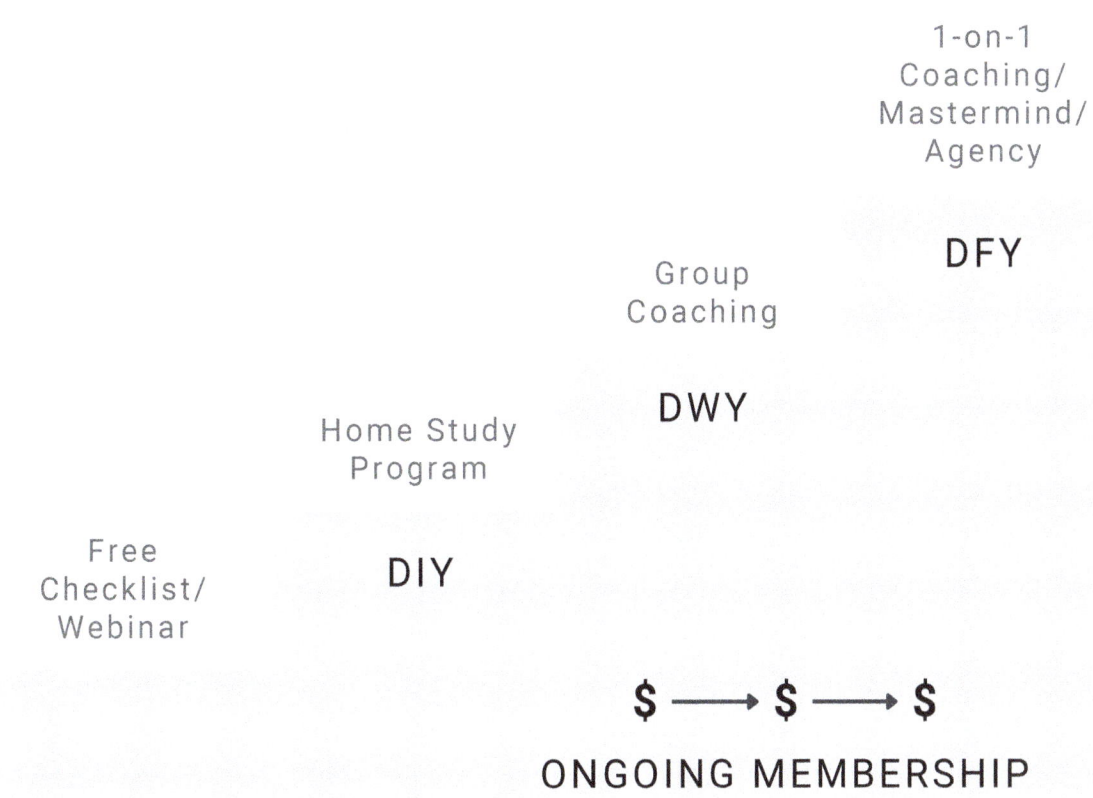

THE VALUE LADDER
FOR A DENTIST

VALUE ↑

- Cosmetic Work
- Dental Work
- Teeth Whitening
- Free Teeth Cleaning

$ → $ → $
6-MONTH CHECKUP

PRICE →

THE VALUE LADDER
FOR A CHIROPRACTOR

VALUE ↑

- Free Exam/Massage
- Spinal Adjustments
- Wellness Care
- Wellness Coaching

$ → $ → $
MONTHLY ADJUSTMENTS

PRICE →

THE VALUE LADDER
FOR BOOKKEEPER

VALUE ↑

- Free Checklist
- Business Evaluation
- Train YOU to use QB
- Quarterly Check-up
- Do All Your Bookkeeping

$ → $ → $

MONTHLY MAINTENANCE PROGRAM

PRICE →

IDEAS FOR
YOUR VALUE LADDER

LEAD MAGNET/FREEBIE

ENTRY PRODUCT

NEXT LEVEL PRODUCT

HIGH LEVEL PRODUCT

THE VALUE LADDER

FOR _____

VALUE ↑

- FREEBIE
- DIY
- DWY
- DFY

$ → $ → $
(Continuity Program)

→ **PRICE**

DIY - Do It Yourself   **DWY** - Done With You   **DFY** - Done For You

NOTES

SECTION FOUR
workbook

GETTING READY TO LAUNCH

STEP BY STEP
MODULE 6

Dynamic Business Building © 2023

THE BETA LAUNCH

THE OFFER - THE NAME
ORGANIC MARKETING AND THE LAUNCH

SECTION INTRODUCTION

In this "Beta Launch" section, we have four important areas to cover. There are separate worksheets for each and it gives you a chance to be creative and have some fun with your topic or niche.

FIRST we have you brainstorm your offer. That is, think about every way that you can add VALUE to your offer, so that it becomes irresistible. WHY? Because you don't want your course to be just another product on the shelf, you want it to stand out as the most amazingly valuable course in the marketplace.

SECOND you will work through a few exercises to choose a name for your course. You decide the emotion, the style, the feeling you want to evoke with your course name. It's good to create a few choices, and see which ones work best for you.

THIRD is all about Organic Marketing. That means marketing that doesn't cost you any advertising dollars! You will work through what "conversation starters" you will use, to create interest in your course. Then you will learn how to multiply the content you already have, so you never run out of things to "talk" about on social media and the rest of the marketplace.

FOURTH is all about the LAUNCH. Not with fancy sales letters or complicated funnels, instead we begin by using the everyday technology that you are familiar with and the people who are already a part of your world. People you know through things like: email lists, social media followers, groups or clubs you belong to, networking that you already take part in, and your friends and family too.

Enjoy each section as it builds toward the completion of your very own online course!

LESSON ONE

BRAINSTORMING YOUR OFFER

MARY AND TEEKWA'S SAMPLE BRAINSTORMING SHEET
FOR A START-UP BUSINESS COURSE

This is where you BRAINSTORM to make your OFFER Irresistible!
The way you make it irresistible, is by adding SO much value, that it becomes a no-brainer to purchase.

There are 4 categories that we want you to brainstorm in: **PHYSICAL, WRITTEN, SPOKEN, and OTHER**

Use our example as a guide, and think of EVERYTHING you can offer under that category that would **enhance the VALUE** of your product, service, or course.

There are no right or wrong answers, these are just ideas, so write them down as you think of them - NO JUDGEMENT. You can assess them later and decide if and when you will use them in your offers.

The next page is yours to fill in with all of your great ideas :)

PHYSICAL

- Actual book
- Notebook
- Course – CD's/Workbook
- Flash cards – 1 lesson or tip/day
- Journal
- Virtual assistance
- Monthly report
- T-shirt as gift
- Reusable bags
- Tool box
- Starter kit-open video w/prize
- Box of stuff
- Recorded interviews

WRITTEN

- What to write – scripts, headlines
- E-book
- Blog
- Checklist, templates
- Swipe files
- Guides
- 30-day start-up guide
- Kindle Books
- IG and FB profiles
- Power point slides
- Bonus courses
- 7-day FB ads +/or FB Live challenge
- What to look for in Bank Acct each day
- Free email course
- Email referral
- Quiz on course to see their level
- Postcards
- Ripl and Canva
- Report on how to work with a VA
- Trello board
- Multiple steps to _____
- 10 Reasons to do FB Live
- Create systems (marketing, hiring)
- How to collaborate with each other

SPOKEN

- Workshop on location (organizer gets something)
- Lunch and learn
- In person classes
- Done With You workshop
- Course on Canva
- Course on Ripl
- Audiobook in any language (Spanish)
- Interviews (downloadable)
- Behind the Scenes
- Video demos
- Video tips -as emails, texts and messenger
- Podcasts

OTHER

- FB Group
- Private FB group
- One-on-One coaching
- Group coaching
- Small Workshops in your home/office
- Affiliates
- YouTube mini-course Free
- YouTube Channel Then YouTube
- Livestream course - paid
- Live training-Free Then invite to Paid course

BRAINSTORMING YOUR OFFER
WORKSHEET

YOUR TURN - BRAINSTORMING SHEET - NO EDITING YOUR IDEAS...YET!

WHAT CAN YOU ADD TO YOUR OFFER TO MAKE IT IRRESISTIBLE?

PHYSICAL
Actual book
Notebook

WRITTEN
Checklist
Ebook

SPOKEN
Workshop
Webinar

OTHERS
1-on-1 Coaching
FB Group

LESSON TWO

NAMING YOUR OFFER

WHAT'S IN A NAME?
If you don't have cool/sexy/clever names, your product /course won't sell as well.
So now you need to come up with fun names for your main offer, cool names for bonuses, even cool names for your modules or the pieces of your offer.

HERE ARE A FEW WAYS YOU CAN BRAINSTORM NAMES!
1-What emotions/feelings are you trying to evoke?
- Sexy, Edgy, Fringe, Hacker, Underground, Mysterious
- Classic, Stable, Trustworthy, Academic, Certified, Expert
- Feminine, Beautiful, Exquisite, Breathtaking, Alluring
- Perfect, Analytical, Clear, Precise, Exacting, Systematic, Logical
- Masculine, Strong, Powerful, Protective, Defender
- Speed, Flexibility, **Dynamic**, Agile, Tone
- On-the-Offense, Aggressive, Bold, Polarizing, Dominant
- Funny, Lighthearted, Comical, Free, Whimsical, Crazy, Colorful

2-Then think about the words that people associate with products....
- System, Bootcamp, Masterclass, Workshop, Program, Course, **Challenge**
- Book, Bundle, Guide, Report, Blackbox, Curriculum
- Membership, Club, Elite, Inner Circle, Mastermind, Posse, Nation, Clan
- Toolkit, Box, Swipes, Templates

3-Then you'll need to think about words associated with your industry.
- Accounting
- Publishing
- Epoxy resin
- Proofreading
- Vitamins/supplements
- Yoga
- **Business**
- Your specific product
- Teacher
- Training
- Belly binding
- Writing
- Social media
- Quick books
- Childbirth
- Energy medicine
- Artwork
- Online business
- AirBnB
- Chiropractic
- Pet supplies
- Pets
- Cremains
- Real Estate
- Heath
- etc

4-Then circle one or two words from sections 1-2-3 and put them together
From there, you can come up with some great names.
Create a few, even if you don't need them right away, it's good to have a few names at your Fingertips ;) Mix and match and have fun!

Once you have a name for your offer, go to GoDaddy and see if the domain name is available. If you love it and are sure, buy the domain (around $10/year). Get the .com, that is the best one for business.

If you already own the domain (or it's attached to a website already), just buy something similar. If you have a funnel, you will want to run it on it's own domain, for tracking purposes.

OUR EXAMPLES:
Dynamic Business Building Challenge
Dynamic Business Building for the Up and Coming Female Tycoon

NAMING YOUR OFFER
WORKSHEET

YOUR TURN!
So now you need to come up with fun names for your main offer, cool names for bonuses, even cool names for your modules or the pieces of your offer.

Circle one or two words from sections 1-2-3 and put them together
From there, you can come up with some great names.
Create a few, even if you don't need them right away, it's good to have a few names at your Fingertips ;) Mix and match and have fun!

HERE ARE A FEW WAYS YOU CAN BRAINSTORM NAMES!

1-What emotions/feelings are you trying to evoke?
- Sexy, Edgy, Fringe, Hacker, Underground, Mysterious
- Classic, Stable, Trustworthy, Academic, Certified, Expert
- Feminine, Beautiful, Exquisite, Breathtaking, Alluring
- Perfect, Analytical, Clear, Precise, Exacting, Systematic, Logical
- Masculine, Strong, Powerful, Protective, Defender
- Speed, Flexibility, Dynamic, Agile, Tone
- On-the-Offense, Aggressive, Bold, Polarizing, Dominant
- Funny, Lighthearted, Comical, Free, Whimsical, Crazy, Colorful

2-Then think about the words that people associate with products….
- System, Bootcamp, Masterclass, Workshop, Program, Course, Challenge
- Book, Bundle, Guide, Report, Black box, Curriculum
- Membership, Club, Elite, Inner Circle, Mastermind, Posse, Nation, Clan
- Toolkit, Box, Swipes, Templates

3-Then you'll need to think about words associated with your industry.
- Accounting
- Publishing
- Epoxy resin
- Proofreading
- Vitamins/supplements
- Yoga
- Business
- Your specific product
- Teacher
- Training
- Belly binding
- Writing
- Social media
- Quick books
- Childbirth
- Energy medicine
- Artwork
- Online business
- AirBnB
- Chiropractic
- Pet supplies
- Pets
- Cremains
- Real Estate
- Heath, etc

Add some of your own industry words:

4-Then jot down a few words from each section - get creative - mix and match and have fun!

Section 1: _____

Section 2: _____

Section 3: _____

Posible Names: _____

_____

_____

LESSON THREE

ORGANIC (FREE) MARKETING

MARKETING DOESN'T HAVE TO COST A LOT OF MONEY
GPS CONVERSATION STARTERS *(As taught by Rachel Miller)*

Choose 1 question from Day 1 and post it on your Facebook profile and page. Notice who answers and what they say. Interact with them and keep the conversation going. Then repeat the same for Day 2 and 3.

DAY 1 (CHOOSE ONE)

Raise your virtual hand if you are a _____!
Raise your virtual hand if you are a small business owner!

You know you're a _____when you _____.
You know you are a gardening lover when you can't resist pulling weeds!

You know you're a _____ when you experience _____ over and over again.
You know you're a mom of a toddler when you experience endless giggles and complete exhaustion, over and over again.

What's your best tip for _____?
What's your best tip for getting your garden ready for spring?
What's your best tip for dealing with the stress of taxes?

What is the one thing that people always come to you for advice about? _____
How do you always put such a great outfit together?

DAY 2 (CHOOSE ONE)

What are you using to (solve) _____?
What are you using to create consistent social media posts?
What are you using to keep track of your finances?

What's your best alternative to _____?
What's your best alternative to snacking for energy in the afternoon?

Who's got a victory in _____? Let's celebrate it!
Who's got a victory in perfecting their handstand? Let's celebrate it!

If you could wave a magic wand and fix one thing about _____, what would it be?
If you could wave a magic wand and fix one thing about your curb appeal, what would it be?
If you could wave a magic wand and change one thing about your appearance, what would it be?
If you could wave a magic wand and change one thing about your finances, what would it be?

Which would you rather - _____ or _____?
Which would you rather - bring your dog to the groomer or groom them yourself?

What is your biggest issue/problem with _____?
What is your biggest issue with finding time for yourself?
What's your biggest problem with creating healthy meals every night?

LESSON THREE

ORGANIC (FREE) MARKETING

DAY 3 (CHOOSE ONE) PROMOTE YOUR STUFF

Hey there! I just created a _____ and it's amazing! Let me know who wants it?
Hey there! I just created a course on Creating Social Media Posts Quickly and Easily and it's amazing! Let me know who wants it?
I just created a course on How to Get the Biggest Tax Refund Possible this year, and it's super simple!!! Who wants it?

If I created a _____, would you want it?
If I created a short cheat sheet on 5 simple things you can do to start your day with energy…naturally, would you want it?
If I created a short video on how to choose the right tax filing status … would you want it?
If I created a short course on how to create a week of healthy meals in just 3 hours … would you want it?

There are X# of things that make the difference between _____ and _____, want to know what they are?
There are 7 things that make the difference between a focused child and a hyper child, want to know what they are?
There are 3 things that make the difference between paying more taxes and getting a refund, want to know what they are?

There are X# of _____ things that _____, who wants to know them?
There are 7 TOP things to do for brake-stopping curb appeal, who wants to know them?
There are 5 simple things you can do to get a bigger tax refund, want to know what they are?

☑ CHECK OFF THE QUESTIONS YOU WANT TO USE

Write down some of your clients' pain points and desires below.
Make the questions specific to YOUR Niche/Ideal Client.
Then follow the steps in Lesson 4 - Launching "Almost" Tech Free - to get the word out!

Your Niche/Target market _____

_____

Their Problems/Pain Points _____

_____

_____

Your Solution/Their Desires _____

_____

_____

ORGANIC (FREE) MARKETING-CONTINUED

> Remember this from "The Client Journey" p54?
> Now we are going to **USE IT IN YOUR ORGANIC MARKETING**
> ...see how on the next page...

**EVERY STEP AND EVERY SUB-STEP
BECOMES A PIECE (OR PIECES) OF CONTENT**

Take each piece of content and create a post about it.
Example: Create a post about the different types of home staging

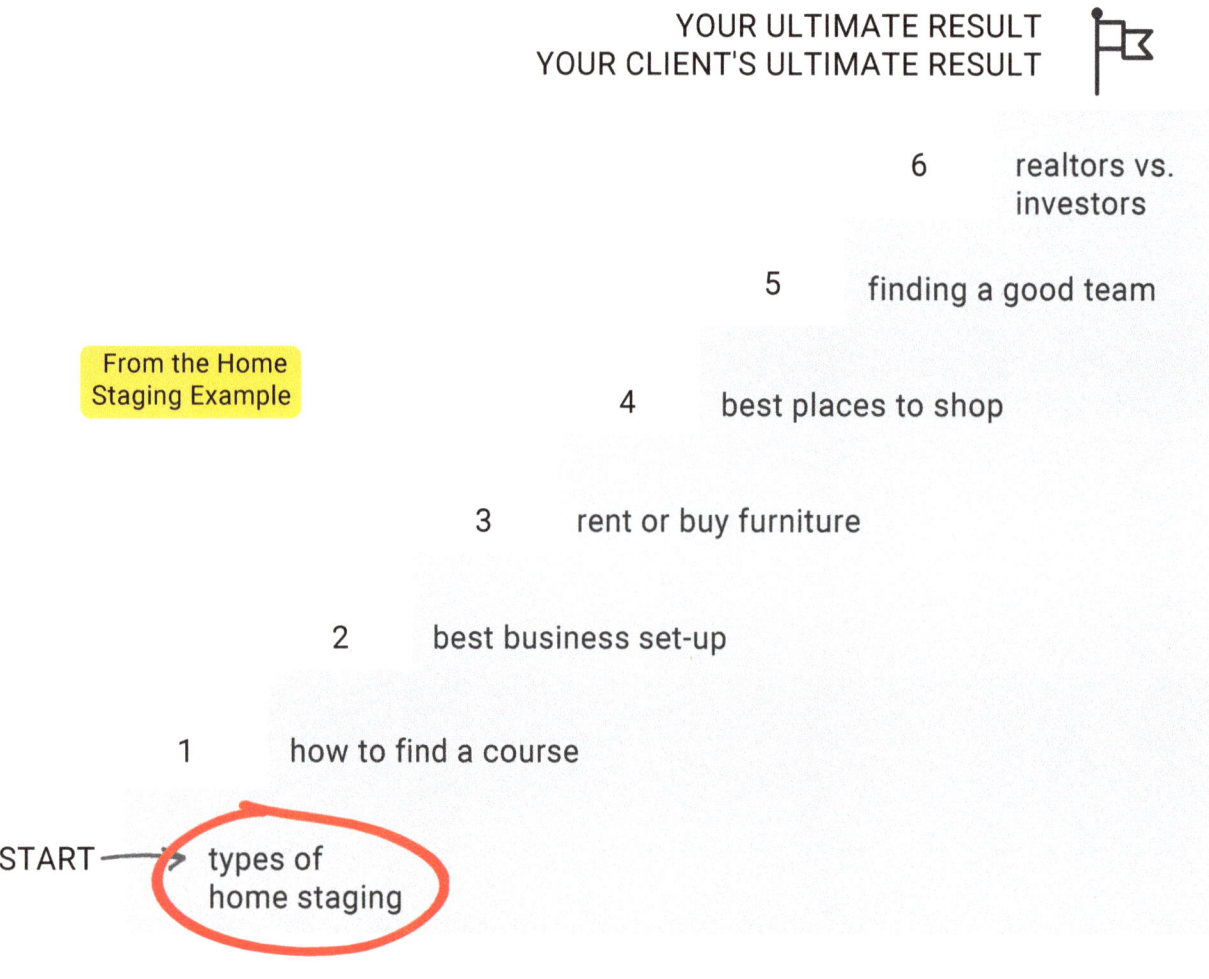

YOUR ULTIMATE RESULT
YOUR CLIENT'S ULTIMATE RESULT

6   realtors vs. investors
5   finding a good team
4   best places to shop
3   rent or buy furniture
2   best business set-up
1   how to find a course
START → types of home staging

From the Home Staging Example

THEN TAKE THE STEPS AND "SUPER SIZE" THEM USING THE
CONTENT MULTIPLIER

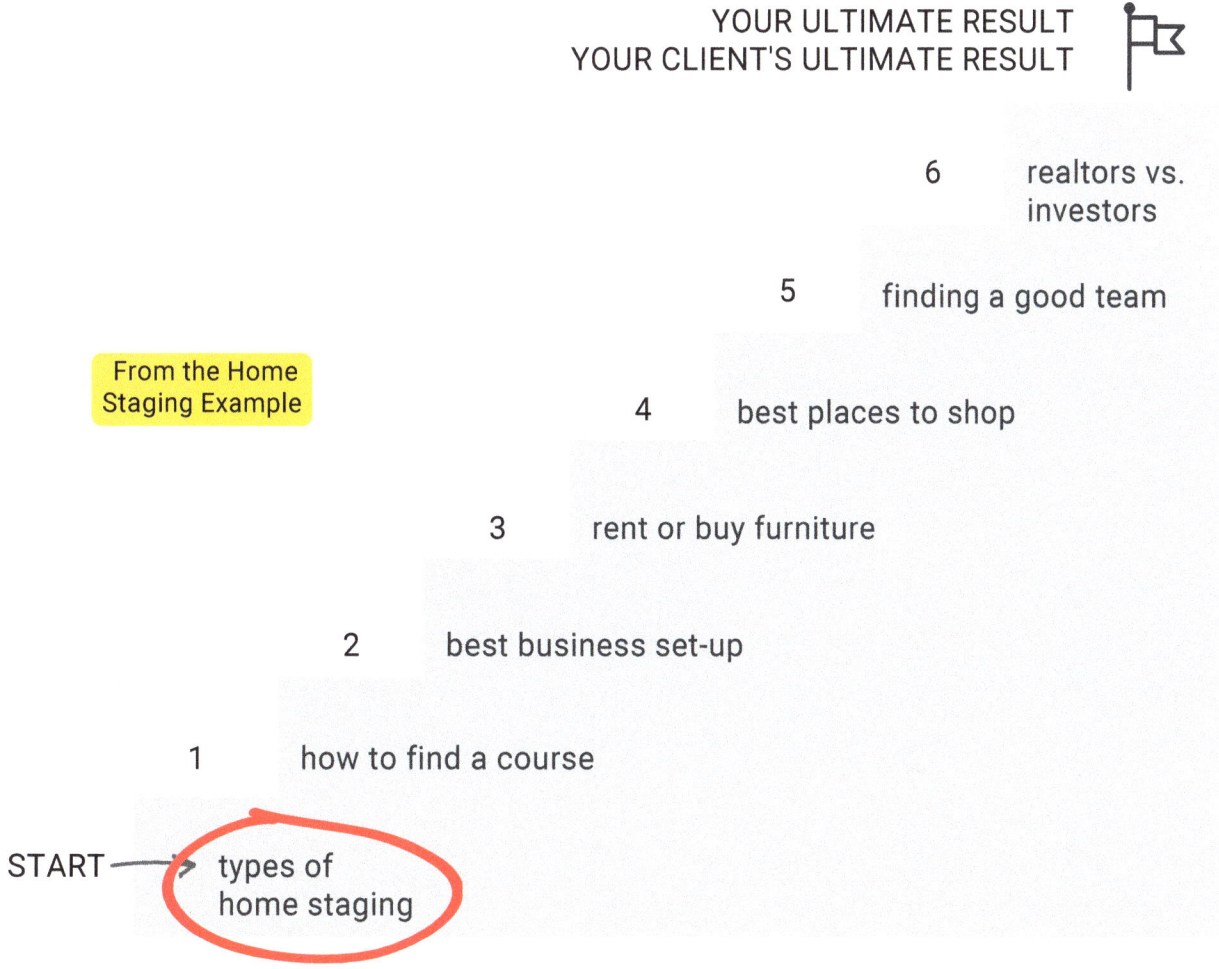

Now..take each piece of content and create 3 different posts from it:
(As taught by Rachel Miller)

1 - Quote or Story about it
Create a text post about the different types of home staging

2 - Picture showing what it is
Create a post with PICTURES of the different types of home staging

3 - Video about it
Create a video of each type of staging - talking about the pros and cons of each

> Here is another example of
> **SIMPLE CONTENT CREATION**

(As taught by Frank Kern)

1 - WHO do you want to attract? *Busy women who like skin care*

2 - WHAT do they want? *Beautiful skin, rosy color, dewy look, clear, even toned, easy routine*

3 - WHAT problems do they have that you can solve?
(And teach around) (What is causing them NOT to have what they want?)
fine lines, puffiness, dryness, saggy skin, dull look, acne blemishes, dark spots, inconvenient routine

4 - HOW do they get it? *Your new skin care line*

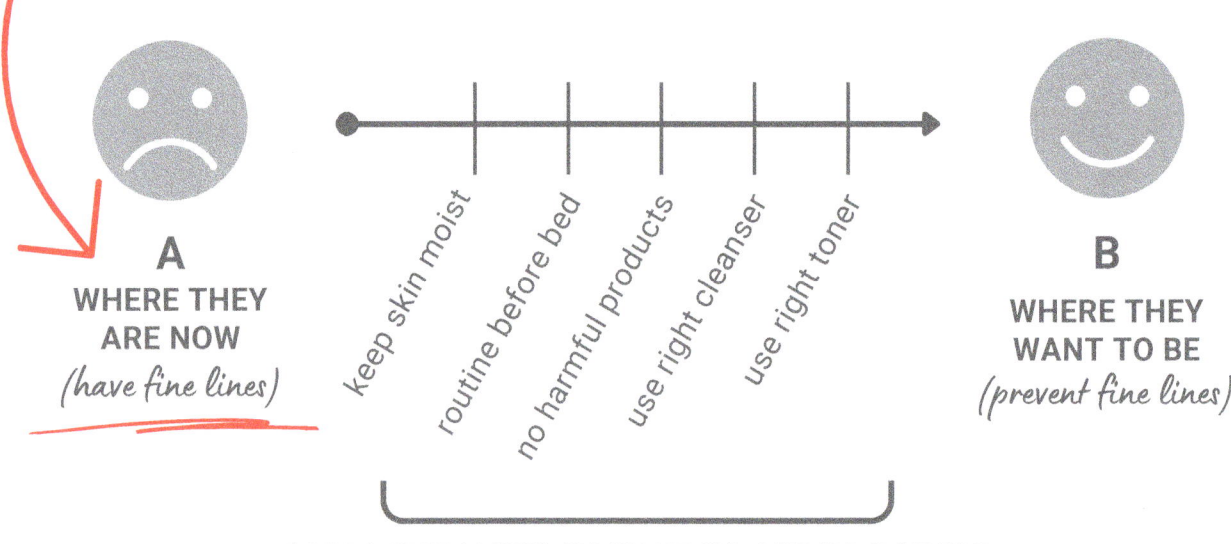

A WHERE THEY ARE NOW *(have fine lines)*

keep skin moist · routine before bed · no harmful products · use right cleanser · use right toner

B WHERE THEY WANT TO BE *(prevent fine lines)*

STEPS THEY NEED TO TAKE TO GET TO POINT B

Chart it out... then take 1, 2 or 3 of these things that are related or work together or make sense together and talk about them in a video.
Repeat the process for each of the problems that you can solve.
This will give you lots to talk about and some great **intent-based branding content videos** to help build your **INVISIBLE LIST!**

LESSON FOUR

LAUNCHING YOUR BETA COURSE - "ALMOST" TECH FREE

Start with the people you know and like and/or have a connection with already:
- Family and Friends First
- People you send Holiday cards to
- Other people in your Social Media network (e.g. Facebook, Instagram, Linkedin, Pinterest, Clubhouse, Tiktok, Youtube, etc...)
- Existing email list
- Existing customers or clients
- Facebook Profile (Your personal page)
- Facebook Business Page
- Facebook Group (Yours)
- Facebook Groups you are a member of (if allowed - ask permission)
- People in your network OFFLINE (Chamber of Commerce, Clubs, Associations, Book clubs,
- Networking groups, Play groups, Social Clubs, etc...)

Use the following page to jot down your contacts to connect with.

*****You only want about 6 - 8 people to start with in your Beta Course!*

Now... Invite them to take your course
- Send an email, text or snail mail to your respective lists - or make a phone call, if you'd like.
- Ask them to spread the word to anyone they might know who could benefit from your course.
- Use your social media platforms to post about your upcoming course - VIDEO is best. choose what you are familiar (notice I didn't say comfortable :) with. Facebook lives, Instagram lives, stories and reels, Youtube videos and shorts, Clubhouse rooms, etc...)
- Message them or have them message you, DM, PM, Back channel, etc...
- Collect their emails (if you don't already have them).
- Collect the money (via paypal, venmo, stripe, cashapp, credit card, or ordinary check, etc...)

Teaching The Course Live
- Teach the course by module, Live with Zoom and make sure to record it.
- Keep each Zoom class short - shoot for less than an hour. (Free Zoom is up to 40 minutes).
- Create a Private Facebook Group (You can teach the course Live in your private Facebook Group, but the only interaction will be through the comments. That is why we recommend Zoom).
- Upload the recording to the FB Group, for those who missed it live, or want to watch it again.
- Organize videos and documents into Guides.
- Highly recommend LIVE Q&A on Zoom as well, each week or every other week.

Have fun and get your students some great results!
(Then get their testimonials :)

WHO WILL I TELL ABOUT MY COURSE

Jot down the names, groups, etc...that you will "Invite" to take your course.

SECTION FIVE
workbook

VALUABLE RESOURCES

CONCLUSION

WHAT'S NEXT

Congratulations!

Whew...you made it, *and we are so proud of you!*

Just think back to when you weren't the author of your very own online course ;)
It is amazing what you have accomplished in such a short time. CELEBRATE your success. And please SHARE your success in the Facebook Group, we all want to celebrate with you.

You can rest a little bit, but we don't want you to stop here. From the very beginning, our goal has been to not only help you create a course...but to create a business. You have done the hard part, now everything can springboard from here, and we can help you, whenever you are ready.

BUT...If you are ready now to go a little deeper into this course creation world, or want to learn how to automate things so you can leverage your time, or maybe you just want to hang out with us a bit more...we have an opportunity for you to do so. (But of course you knew we would!)

It's called the **Course Creation GPS Plus+**. This is a monthly live, interactive coaching program where we serve YOU in just the areas that you need it the most. If you have questions about some of the information you learned in the course, we will answer them. If you need more clarification on a process, we can help you out. If you just want to keep going so that you can take your course, and your new online business, to the next level...we are here for you.

If you have any interest, or need a few questions answered before you make a decision, send us an email @ **info@dynamicbusinessbuilding.com** to set up a time to chat via zoom, to see if this is a good fit.

No matter what your decision, we have thoroughly enjoyed spending this time with you, in-person or through video. We know there are many opportunities and options out there and we want to THANK YOU for investing in yourself through our course. Here's to your continued success...

Teekwa and Mary

TOOLS &RESOURCES

TO HELP GET IT DONE RIGHT

THE COURSE CREATION GPS

- **ZOOM.COM** Live video conference platform where you can teach and record your course.
- **FACEBOOK.COM** A free platform to host your course materials and interact with students.

THE CREATIVE

- **CANVA.COM** Make beautiful posts for Social Media and printable materials.
- **WORDSWAG.CO** Also good for making simple yet elegant posts for Social Media - APP via Playstore or App Store.
- **RIPL.COM** Create amazing videos from pictures in just a few minutes - App via Playstore or App Store.

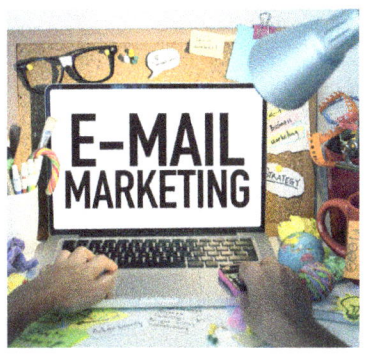

THE CONTACT & FOLLOW UP

- **MAILCHIMP.COM** Free service for creating email lists and campaigns.
- **MAILERLITE.COM** Free service for creating email lists and campaigns.

EXTRA HELP

- **FIVERR.COM** Help with anything you want/need to outsource.
- **POWERPROASSISTANTS.COM** Virtual Assistants for your organizational or technological needs.
- Join Our Facebook Group **LADY TYCOONS**

RESOURCES
TO HELP GET IT DONE RIGHT

Use this space to jot down any other resources we mention in the course that you may find helpful.

NOTES

NOTES

"If there's a course that you want to take, but it hasn't been created yet, then you must create it."

WHAT OUR WONDERFUL CLIENTS HAVE TO SAY

She helped me to walk through this whole thing... she does an amazing job ... she helped me to walk through this whole thing of how to promote my pre-recorded yoga material online and to get people interested through Instagram, Facebook, and even Clubhouse, which I had no clue about. She's just an amazing resource, has so much knowledge and you should check out how she's helping people to do their courses online. Thank you so much!

-Raji Thron

Yoga Master, Teacher trainer and Author

Mary and Teekwa take you through, step-by-step...
... through all of the building blocks, you need to build a successful online business. From the comfort of your own home, you too can learn to build your own online business.
I did - you can too...you won't be disappointed.

-Linda Conti

Pet grooming salon and Pet retail shop owner

You will learn a lot of very interesting things...
...with Dynamic Business Building, I have two lovely hosts, Mary and Teekwa and the first thing I learned was Canva. I never heard of Canva before - now I've heard of Canva. So, you will learn a lot of very interesting things that you never heard of before, or I have anyhow, and thanks ladies.

-Michelle Rudolph

Rieki master and Seimei practitioner

Thank you for a great Dynamic Business course...
Thanks Mary and Teekwa. Thank you for a great Dynamic Business course. I just wanted to show my appreciation and thank you.

-Felicia Arago

Decorative painting and design, Hand painted furniture

You fulfilled all the promises that you offered in the beginning of the class and more...
Thanks, Teekwa and Mary, for creating such a great online class – TO CREATE an online class. And so you promised in four to five weeks that we'd be able to create, in this course creation GPS class, an online class that we could launch for ourselves and you sure did it! You helped to facilitate, with all of your knowledge and wisdom and your kindness and enthusiasm. And thank you so much, I look forward to launching that class. You fulfilled all of the promises that you offered in the beginning of the class and more, and once again thanks.

-Rose Fitzgerald

Transformational body work, Trauma release exercises, (TRE)

The course I took before seemed a little confusing...
Many years ago, I took a course on how to market on Facebook...the course took seemed to be a little confusing, to access the tools to get a professional-looking Facebook page. The other day I came across Dynamic Business Building...they took you through, step-by-step, how to put together a professional Facebook page for marketing. I appreciate the time Mary and Teekwa have put together, answering questions, providing you with the tools, and making it much easier to handle. Thanks.

-Gina Haber

Quick Book advisor and Accountant

HAVE QUESTIONS?
Contact Dynamic Business Building
Email: info@dynamicbusinessbuilding.com

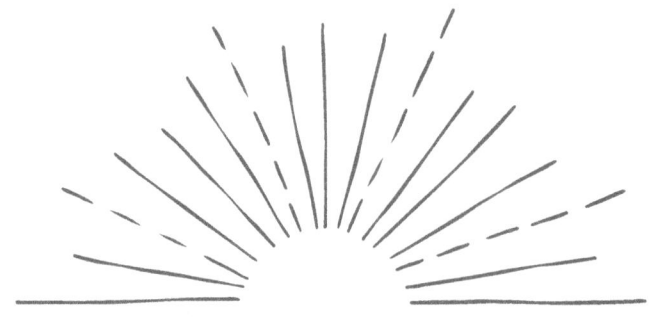

THE FUTURE BELONGS TO THOSE WHO BELIEVE IN THE BEAUTY OF THEIR DREAMS.

- ELEANOR ROOSEVELT

www.ingramcontent.com/pod-product-compliance
Lightning Source LLC
Chambersburg PA
CBHW042353070526
44585CB00028B/2914